LEONEL ROQUE

LEONEL ROQUE

JIM SMITH

COTEAU BOOKS

Thanks to Curbstone Books and Sandy Taylor for permission
to publish translations of Leonel and Roque.

Edited by Geoffrey Ursell
Cover design by Minal Kharkar, Pixel Communications.
Book design by Duncan Campbell.
Cover painting "Exit" by Mindy Camponeschi, 1996.
Author photo by Douglas Young, 1997.

Coteau Books acknowledges the financial support of: the Government of Canada through the Canada Council for the Arts and the Department of Canadian Heritage Book Publishing Industry Development Program; the Government of Saskatchewan through the Saskatchewan Arts Board; and the City of Regina through the Regina Arts Commission, for our publishing activities.

Coteau Books celebrates the 50th Anniversary of the Saskatchewan Arts Board, and the 40th Anniversary of the Canada Council for the Arts with this publication.

Canadian Cataloguing in Publication Data

Smith, Jim
Leonel/Roque

Poems.
ISBN 1–55050–128–3

I. Rugama, Leonel, 1949–1970   —Poetry
2. Dalton, Roque, 1935–1975   —Poetry   I. Title.

PS8587.M545   L46   1998   C811'.54   C98–90012–4

c

Coteau Books
401-2206 Dewdney Avenue
Regina, Saskatchewan
Canada   S4R 1H3

AVAILABLE IN THE U.S. FROM:

General Distribution Services
85 River Rock Road, Suite 202
Buffalo, New York
USA   14207

THE STATE OF
EMERGENCY LAWS

The state
dreams
the citizens
it would like

to have

CONTENTS

II. HERE

III. LEONEL

IV. ROQUE

PREFACE

This book bears, in part, a relation to certain "real life" lives and "historical" events which needs explanation. The Leonel of the title refers to Leonel Rugama, a young Sandinista poet who at 20 years old was killed in a shootout with Nicaragua's National Guard in January 1970, almost ten years prior to the Sandinista victory. At the time of his death he had published a few stunning poems; a single posthumous volume was one of the first books published in post-Somoza Nicaragua, and remains in print today. The Roque of the title refers to Roque Dalton of El Salvador, who at 40 years of age, and with a substantial writing career and numerous publications, was murdered by unknown members of his own revolutionary party in San Salvador in May 1975. The circumstances and the tragedy of his murder are still hotly debated today within certain Salvadoran circles. Both men were poets firmly committed to an intense political struggle. This struggle claimed each of their lives.

Leonel/Roque is not a history, nor is it a biography, nor a political tract, though, as serial poem sequence, it occasionally exercises its right to take on aspects of any of these. It is, perhaps, a distant relative of the Latin American genre of *testimonio,* in that a number of voices testify about events and experiences which arise from the latter part of this tormented century.

The Spanish expressions and phrases scattered throughout the work are explained in a brief glossary. Short notes on some people and places mentioned are gathered together as well following the glossary.

The book ends with a small selection of my translations of certain neglected works by each writer. When forgetting is a weapon used us by those who continually rewrite history, remembering is an act of self-defence.

I.
THERE

LEONEL (EARLY)

In the *barrio* (that one night we whispered would someday be named after Dolores Estrada) several *compañeros* showed me their poems, heat still rising from them, shavings of rough-stubbed pencil down the side of the page, and by the literary standards of the empire – subject to any aesthetic aside from a feel for the sweat and *dolor* they suffered – these carven objects might have been less impressive. What I am saying is that T.S. Eliot and Walt Whitman might not have been impressed. But the fact that the air was pungent with burning rubber and woodsmoke, that the *guardia* had made three sweeps in this area alone within the last seven days, taking six people, one a friend, the fact that sweat shone on the face of one of the writers, and that they knew I was a poet of a rather confusing notoriety, that sweat...it was too much, it was just enough, it reduced the need for foreign judgement, it was a poem, an object as homey as a carven wooden toy handed to a child and the child smiles and knows what it is it represents. Fuck, man, there is no experience like it, I tell you, there is no way that any *hijo de puta* is going to take that page from the hand of my *compañero*. It will be there in his hand until *he* decides what to do with it – rewrite it, send it to the papers, or put it with a pile of other papers and show it on a Tuesday like this to his grandchild, saying, this, this is the poem that I shared with the poet Leonel Rugama of Nicaragua, and I have always been proud of it and have never had to hide it.

We sat in a circle, a rough circle, the asses of our pants dirty from the earth around us.

We were coated in earth and it never stopped getting thicker, and the *ron* ran out early, and no one had any *cordobas* to buy any more, and we were all thirsty as hell, and I was supposed to be early in the Mercado Oriental tomorrow to pass a message, but that poem, and the other poems, shedding awkwardness like light and making a virtual pile of pencil shavings at my feet, well fuck it all, man, fuck it all, these were the times that made being a poet right for *me*, and we all knew we were in a country that might be something someday, only if some of us would live to live in it.

We are both still alive. Yet it is taken for granted that our mail is opened by others, read by others and disposed of. Does it make you want to scream, as I do? After all, this is the throat of the Americas, even if they treat it like the toilet's bowl. Surveillance – always to be under surveillance. How do we come to cope with it? Every day someone we know is picked up, and taken to the edge of the city, where the garbage builds up in heaps, and they are hacked into pieces, or kicked into the other world (wherever that might be), and usually their hands are cut off – do you ever sit in the heat and imagine what it actually feels like to have a machete descend through the flesh and the muscle and the tendon and finally the bone and through flesh again – and there they lie until some kid comes along and watches the flies. My vision of those flies is a horde of little green *guardia*, buzzing and attacking and consuming and laying their evil eggs. In someone we know. Over and over and over again, every day that we live.

This we must endure, the certainty there will be a day when it's us on the floor of that car or that jeep and on the way to that place that smells. My *compañera* asks me why I carry a gun if I am a poet and if I am searched it will mean the end. You know why don't you? We both know, and it was Rigoberto Lopez Perez helped teach us the value of arms here in the throat of the Americas. When I write, it is the words themselves, every one of the words, so unlike the *guardia* flies, which ask me whether...well, I am not at all sure what it is that they ask. That is part of the struggle, and part of the presence I feel outside the door of this hut in the *barrio*. I am enclosing a pamphlet.

Leonel

FISICAMENTE

You may never see your brain.
Orders are given,
a suggestion made,
and part of you dies.
The brain will resist
the peaceful
transferral of power.
It is not progressive.
There are endless small and unremarked
crimes which happen nightly,
sorrow is localized
then exterminated
in the far-flung colonies
the body.

The heart, yes, the heart
might make an impassioned plea –
¡cese la represión! –
but in the conference rooms
of the mighty brain,
there is nothing but cynical laughter,
and no odour, no taste
no sensation at all
as the fingers die
and the toes die.

The brain is staging its yearly fiesta
all the noblest thoughts are there
the brain toasts its successful
containment policy.

As the lights are extinguished
somewhere in the distance
a voice
cries out.

Why do we bother writing to each other? So that a letter finally gets there and sits because the other has been murdered? Because in the composition we explain our ideas to ourselves? Because you will die, I will die, they will die and it will or will not make a jot of difference in the world around us, and we want some record to be available someday that we were indeed on one side or the other? I have learned so very much from reading your booklet, that there is no difference between our struggles, in one sense, and that there is a world of difference in another, or many others. You have Sandino, we have Farabundo Marti. Virtually the same year, they died, were murdered. Our *matanza* stole how many lives, 35,000? You have lost the same number in the course of more years.

Do we write then because we are the same person, grown up only several hundred miles apart, carrying out a doppelgänger life in which the same character gets to do different things but within a limited frame? As I close the doors and pull the shutters on my mother's house, lift the material from its place in the corner and begin to tune the shortwave, do you speak nervously around the corners of your mother's house, and approach the corner where you unearth a poem?

Will my next letter tell you of a broadcast that I heard, or will one never arrive? Will your next enclose a poem or two, or blank sheets?

Why when I thought of you last night did I see myself?

Is the knock on the door innocent?

There are so many questions.

Others die. Because of our actions, independent of our actions, or worse, in spite of our actions.

The living need us. As long as we do not forget the dead.

Con un abrazo fuerte

Roque

THE LITTLE BIRD

The little bird hides in drink
and in the machete used to lop off an arm

the bird sits right there on the stem
of your neck and whispers
that none of it is real
that none of it matters
that doing one thing is as good as
doing another
and doing nothing is just as good
as either

this damn bird
it sells itself to you
through fear
or through
your own grand desire
to become drunk
and listen to a song
you don't hear

he became drunk
he was pushed into a black International jeep
and pushed out again at the side of a road
with nobody on it
where three slugs were put into his
heart, his head and his balls
before his arm was
lopped off
and thrown away into the field

a totally random action
like the high note
in the little bird's song
as it sings
drunken
that nothing matters
that
it is all
the same

I never had the chance to hear *Guitarra Armada*'s songs about how to clean your gun, set to the music popular in my town, sung by my friends who outlived me to circles that widened until they included my whole nation.

I did hear the sound of Detroit engines of the trucks as they surrounded the house, and the chop-chop of those splendid U.S. turbines of the helicopter, and the dark crow voices of National Guard officers as they chewed on the problem of three people in a house who wouldn't come out, scratching in their Washington combat fatigues.

I had no time to hear my brother and sister sing in the square in Managua the songs about General Sandino.

I heard instead how bullets from Virginia can splinter wood, and I was able to measure just how much of a wall would crumble at the *crummmmmp* of a grenade manufactured from Pennsylvania steel. It is a sizeable chunk, believe me.

There are always songs you will never hear, so often voices which never reach our ears in time, obscured by sounds no one ever desires to hear. Like the sound of my companions dying, aching to scream over the sound of gunfire that the sounds washing over this house were the sounds of the past, that the future would sound different.

When I cried, *Surrender your mother!* I was thinking of nothing more than how sore my knees were, how the dust of sprayed mortar irritated my eyes, how my arm ached, how loud it all was, how I would project myself to the future in which the Captain's voice with its alien inflection would be just a bad memory.

I heard how my accent was that of my own town, my family, my people.

It was so many miles from his house to his house. One went to one school, one went to another. They first heard of each other at seventeen – Rigoberto seventeen years dead, Leonel seventeen years old. No – that is a lie. Rigoberto killed Somoza the First in 1956; Leonel was killed by the *guardia* in 1970. Fourteen years apart. Thus there existed only six years in which they could meet. Imagine – Nicaragua is a small country and both grew up in Managua. Thus it would have been possible for Leonel, skipping school in which that day he was to learn the fictive history of the so-called bandit Sandino (whom some called the General of Free Men), and walking past the National Palace on his way to the Cine Altamirana – let's say he was five, and it was 1955 – and he passed a real stringbean, a young man with a twisted face from, say, pain, composing a poem to his mother to explain what he thought he might do some day. Leonel didn't care that he had never written a poem, as Rigoberto composed his last, and bought a pistol, which he kept under a pillow filled with straw for nearly six months.

No one saw the child and the youth pass each other. Only Rigoberto heard Leonel shout, for want of anything better to do on one of the hottest days in hot Managua that year, *Hey stringbean, what the fuck do you say, what are you doing?* and similarly, no one saw Rigoberto look sadly upon the child for whom he – so briefly, and then dismissed it – thought he might sacrifice himself for a future that would surely be as bad but that was nonsense, what was the worth, this kid was shit.

But in this lie, if there had been an observer, that observer might have cared to tell some stranger, a kid or a sallow youth, that for a moment in the hottest shadows that year in Managua, someone passed someone else in the street and thought nothing of it, consequences be damned, and one passed on to his house, where his mother waited, and the other passed on to his house, where his mother waited, and both mothers complained that not enough was being done. Both mothers felt their hearts shudder at the sound of helicopters and the boots of the *guardia* right outside their door.

No, they never met. That is less of a lie.

yes, Leonel was all of these:
short, fat, squat and dumpy,
unkempt, dirty, sweaty, rude,
loud, abrasive and quiet,
vulgar and softspoken
as well as being unshorn,
macho and sensitive, indeed
most ladylike in his sensitivity,
thoughtless and caring
by turns
specific and general,
friendly but hostile,
attentive to his mother
and family
while neglecting them,
a friend to those less fortunate
than himself
who lacked these qualities.

None of these
were shield against bullets
none of these
bore on his death
nor had much to do with what poured
from him.

He wrote his *poemas*
late into that night
after throats tired arguing
"strategy"
like angry cicadas
trying to be quiet
and, as he wrote once with a mere stub
of liberated pencil:

he did not talk of dying for his country
no
he just died

like
that

WHERE TO BE FRIGHTENED

They told me never to be frightened
in the hills around Matagalpa.
They never said why, just
that it was the worst
idea of all.

SOUTH

It is good to have guests, of course,
and it is not good to have guests –
you never know when they will come for you.

You never know if when the rug is lifted
a squad of cockroaches will surround you,
a plague of ticks force you
into the heart of the sweating street,
into *their* secret places,
whether mice are tunnelling
in order for your most secret sounds
to reach their quivering ears,
and you never know if the centipede,
Mister Centipede himself,
is marching past your small cone
of vision, you never know
about the ants and their levelling,
but what is more obvious
than the flies with TV camera eyes,
the mosquitoes sampling blood,
the dandruff that sleeps atop your head
only so it can hear your thoughts?

Even as they carry you off, you shout
Why bother asking me anything?
You know it all.

That is the difference
between you.

and when you come to me lachrymose demonstrating how the
bullet passed through your ugly little sheaf of poems,
each molecule of blood spilling from your wounds named
with the name of a hero or a martyr,
your smile full of teeth which, I am sorry, but it is
true, remind me of nothing more than the devastated
silhouette of Managua at dusk,
I see your books dog-eared in the Mercado Oriental, half
submerged in straw hats woven by weeping mothers,
I ask the young man in green fatigues and a face shining
from the sweat of having sat up all night on the curb
protecting his multiply-insufficient *barrio* from generic crime,
I demand of the Bank of America building, proof of earthquakes
and the solidity of dangerous abstraction,
and your own brother who shucked the village then
the region then the very country of your birth
from his shoulders like, well, nothing so much as like a yoke,
I request the very air, the music, the fruits of the
earth of your too humble dress
a simple question
that deals with why and how and when and where and what
and, finally, deals with me,

the answer is equally simple, I guess, I know, I am sure,
and they all answer, in unison of course,
presente!
which, translated, means he is here, means he never left,
means he will always be with us, and so on, you get the drift,
we will never forget you, and all those things
which are said and unsaid and cried out and whispered,
and I find myself
speaking to you
here

THE *POPOL VUH* REPAIR SHOP

Where they don't do such good work, just ask Bartolomeo
        de las Casas,
an angry priest, who saw them take the holy books – in fact,
all the books – which were in the back seat of a civilization,
toss them on a heap and burn them at the end of a hard work day.
You just drive history in, brand new off the lot,
        leave it in their hands, you'll see what I mean

First they'll give you an estimate
scribbled across the august newspaper of record of the day
(words will smear across your trembling hands and dirty
        the first clean thing you touch)
and the figures they'll stand by, if you look at them closely,
wriggle and slide into each other worse than a bad case
of heartworm until you don't know, can't know, the cost

But there ain't a lot of choice, given the complicated stuff
under the hood of history these days, you've always meant
to get a few books and do it yourself, but...

Minutes after you agree that consensus is a good thing
and somehow you have participated in their choice
and it is in their hands, they've unleashed the imps
and before your very eyes the damn thing has disappeared
under a swirl of activity which is convincing but unsettling

There are noises that do not sound healthy, but they are
explained away as a painful but necessary part of a process
that is actually indeed out of their hands and of which
they are as much victims as you, and you're not sure
exactly what this means, but something's getting done
and it's at least better than history sitting out there
on the street with no chance of going anywhere in it

Someone is using a Big Lie© brand hammer to pound some sense
into cylinders of event, somewhere there is a screech
of something being born, then the repeated clang of it dying

And by the time you're on your way back from the battered
pop machine of indulgence, or dangling the oversize key
to the dirtiest washroom of poverty, *No telling how much time
this will take* still echoing in your ears, some expert
hands you the bill and places you behind the wheel
which, you have a faint memory, pointed toward, not away
from the engine, and wasn't there a windshield – oh it's
off that way I see, well, I don't, and it doesn't seem to move
you start to complain just as their best imp swings that
omni-purpose wrench toward what will soon used to be your eyes

THE GLASS BALLOT BOX

either half full
or half empty
of severed thumbs

1.
Having forgotten the miserable ones, we went on...
it is so crowded here in heaven,
no one saw who is hurt, they only are gone home and shrink
into their hurt until they disappear.
So then I said to him *Don't think you are so special.*
When she wormed her way into the heart temple, she saw
several triptychs of her home and lover;
trumpets announce the return of the lost men,
who wore faces of personal relatives who stayed out of life.
No one has decided what they want, but wear on their bodies
signs indicating indifference to wiles gone heavenward.
No one wants none, hearing irrelevance through blank ears,
not character but fear determines whence we flee rightly.

2.
Someone not of our party led us out of there.
Both feared the colours propagating without defined wavelength,
thought having night's bad idea – whence issued a carnival.
First living together then separate, men (word missing)
sensitive women only in unusual circumstance.
Uncertainty spreads undefined by border crowds,
kiss gently more out of circumspection than timidity,
slinking through tunnels older than we,
it is always surprising to discover your name.
Death had claimed their predecessors – Mayans, Aztecs, Pipil,
now the Quiche slide away. Mothers heavy with child keening
walked forestward. They knew. The telling of the tale
by virtue of the intercession of gods falters,
a concretion of her being sent him reeling.
No one can love an other perfectly.
No need to babble of treasures, only to define their parameters.
Hung, the carcass transforms into itself.
Which, remains.

THE GAME

get killed
live in the memory of the people
watch them fight
help when you can
kick at the pricks
offer succour to the wounded
a kind word to a lover
sarcasm to the profound
friendship to those who value it
laugh
laugh as often as possible
at the ridiculousness
of living in a number of memories
never fucking or eating
just like the boys
in the hills
above town
thank god
they're up there
help others remember
there should always be boys
in the hills
when your brother
and your sister never have time
to fuck nor
food to eat
no matter who
– fuck them –
is in charge

and when the boys get into town
support them
any way you can

Just outside the small building which serves as the Museum of the Revolution, a truck-sized mass of melted brass resembles nothing so much as a giant ear, overturned. The day of the Victory, Somoza's self-erected Bolivaroid statue was pulled down and partially melted. It is said he had balked at the cost of a French-produced original, so procured, much cheaper, a U.S. Civil War castoff, replacing its head with a bust of his own. The heat is so intense in the square today I lean my head inside the cavity, where a small piece of shade is hiding. The noise of the Roberto Huembes marketplace recedes. It is almost silent, and further down inside I can see the waxy, necrotic gleam of a small puddle of water, most likely from the day's brief torrential downpour, or yesterday's, or the day before's, who knows how long it has festered there. I breathe in its fetid organic odour. I am dizzy. It is the incessant heat of agitated molecules. It is the stink of a multitude of never-to-be-discovered corpses. It is no longer silent. There is the insistent keening of a procession of the Mothers of the Disappeared at some distance. On my tongue I taste bitter, hopeless tears. The taste sharpens to quinine as my tongue constricts and protrudes. There is sudden pain at the nape of my neck as if a machete had broken skin to hit bone. My head pitches free of clenched shoulders, rolls forward and splashes into the dead lake, sputters bobbing, spitting out an ear-sized turd as dark as a dried plum. The miserly sun is the heel of a shell casing glinting off a long way. I am cold. Other isolate heads bob beside me. I can read lips. They wail that they were the ears of Somoza, that they deserved better than this, that they had no choice and did not do so willingly, but one has to live, eh? I do not want to be near them, paddle awkwardly with my tongue a distance away, gasp for air, it is frigid, the lake is freezing over, a dugout canoe is growing toward me, racing the edge of ice, I close my eyes as I am scooped up, keep them screwed shut until I am tumbled forward on the shore, rolling to jar heavily against my shoulders. When I open my eyes I see sky and a curious child's face. Someone helps me up and I lean on the rigid leg of a bronze horse. I understand enough Spanish to know someone is talking about the stupid yankee, only a stupid yankee could get his head stuck in Somoza's horse's butt. I sit jarringly, rest my head on the statue, watch for my friend who needed so badly to see the Museum one more time.

In one of the meetings, Valdez suggested the collection of those parts of bodies which were unidentifiable from the offal fields where the death squads dumped them, and the sending of them by some circuitous route to the dictator himself.

It was considered seriously and fully discussed.

In the end, we rejected the *compañero's* well-meant proposal since it would mean returning to the monster something which was not his and which he had never had the right to rend apart in the first place.

Valdez understood.

Contra Sutra

1.

selling blood used to be profitable, the hungry
would line up at the gate
to be tapped, and we would fly
it direct to Miami, a good market,
our overhead the lowest,
raw material beating down our door

and it's ruined
we can't get a pint out of the country
and goddamit like any shopkeeper
worth his salt, we'd spill our product
over the entire land
rather than be done out
of a market

easy to understand
for a businessman – if they won't
pay us for the grain or the meat or the oil
or the tools, we'd rather see them go to waste
than be given away for free

fuck them
someday soon
they'll beg
for a rusty needle
an empty bag
a black market

it will be all
right again

2.

you have to see both sides
of the issue, the ambiguity resident
in the skinning of Sandinista militia
bodies which are only bodies
after all, tissue,
sure it's a brain,
but the person is dead aren't they
anyway, left by the pedal
of the coffee-picker's jeep

a war which doesn't even exist
ranks opportunity of the moment
over liberal ethics
doesn't it

these things have been won
or lost on effect.

3.

you are a creature of the marketplace
even if you fidget in the basket
sloppily labelled *these are not creatures
of the marketplace*, I defy you
to step outside a frame of reference
you had nothing to do with
in the first place:

remember this well!

your sperm can be sold,
your womb is rentable,
the newborn fetches a premium,
child labour is valued, your worth
doubles when you enter the relative mainstream
of sexual desire, the energy of youth
can increase production overnight,
at almost any time your body parts
are in short supply – the vendor can
name his own price! – and as for killing you
well, subject to market fluctuations,
it can provide quite a living, and as long
as there are cannibals there's a posthumous
profit to be had, and however you reach such a state,
there are dirt vendors and real estate agents.

multiply this by a shackfull, a crowded *barrio*,
a number of small cities, innumerable villages, countryside,
provinces, and a nation however small.

You will see that the stakes are not inconsiderable,
the gods always hungry.

EARTHQUAKE

Countless victims, buried like sticks,
did not cause the earth to shake,
did not make the Cathedral spin like an epileptic dog,
and it was not the greed of the overclass
sat down like a big fat, heavy box
on the wrong end of a teeter-totter
which threw truckloads of National Guard
like projectile vomit
against Somoza's bunker.

It was just nature, or rather unjust nature
that crushed one of Rosario Murillo's children
so that she would eventually get a poem out of it.
It is a fine poem, but – after all – not a fair trade.

At dawn on December 23, 1972, something bad happened
to Managua, and the city was erased as if by a poet
with a rare awareness of the provisional nature
of that which is built, created, or otherwise
made to exist.

Much that was acquired left without goodbyes, and
it is impossible to judge if the bad lost more
than the good.

Where a city once stood, a city now stands, certainly a bit
usual, as things go. There have been reports that a child
wanders sometimes, crying for a pencil he had seen
in the pocket of a soldier, but it is unclear
as to whether it is Rosario's kid, wanting to erase her poem.
Anyway, the pencil is long gone,
crushed under stone.

After the quake, some woke up
and some didn't. No one can contest that.

INTERVIEW

So what is this about pulling off his testicles?

it had to be done the son of a whore would not talk

About what, exactly?

about who he worked with, names were what we wanted

Suppose for a moment he did not know any names?

that was not possible he was afraid when he saw us so we knew

Maybe he knew you were going to pull his testicles off?

but you are not afraid for nothing there must be a reason

That is what I am saying, he was afraid you would hurt him?

we would not hurt him if he was innocent

How do you know he was not innocent?

why, *puta*, because he got afraid as soon as we'd spotted him

So he was guilty?

that's right obviously he had something on his mind

What did you do with the testicles?

in his mouth

Why?

so people know we mean business

The Little Darling

rough canvas hood
with drawstring
& filled
with quicklime

pulled down rapidly
over the head
while the arms
are pinned
drawstring
pulled tight

Nothing more to it
than that

It is then
highly advisable
to stand back
& watch

from a distance

PRAYER

Oh great teddybear of the left, cushy
inside worker at the heart
of the party organ,
come out, come out, today is Monday,
we start at the foot
of the work week
and climb.

It is time for a new order,
time to jumpstart the revolution,
hotwire the imagination
of the beobabs and heffalumps,
the bambis whose delicate ears
are precious too to the cause.

The weekend of surveillance is over –
mordor's microphones cough out smoke & fumes,
the metallic eyes of the dark lord wobble
on their stalks. They could not believe
their mechanistic senses, what they saw
was clearly impossible.
Ming's troops have all called in sick.

So let us begin again by giving up
our taste for socialist art,
let us start afresh
by dressing up in coloured clothes
& vie with each other
for the funniest praxis.

The prisoners will not disappear
& the tortured will still have to be tortured
for a while,
but they will hear us out here
& know we have not forgotten ourselves

know we are coming for them
making a joyous noise.

AL FRESCO

My head hurts, it is noon,
and an International
with darkened windshield waits
outside on the curb.
Death sits in the cafeteria
with a small purse which contains
a nine-millimetre automatic pistol.
I spend too much on lunch,
did I mention that my head hurts
since this morning,
it is too late for economy.
I stand up to go.
Outside the engine starts.

RANDOM PRICE LIST

For 25 cents, a pamphlet
on how to obtain the (temporary)
favour of the Virgin of Patronage.

For 20 cents, a pen.

And, for 35 cents, someone
will write your letter to
the (damned)
Virgin,

praying that she grant you

the $500.00 (U.S. – of course!)
that will allow you
to leave

this blasted
land.

THE MAP OF THE BODY

Yes, the overlay of the head did seem to fit North America,
swollen but recognizable, given the explanation,
and yes, South America did seem to resemble in a certain way
the body (Paleolithic mother-figure?) turning
on the pirouettish Del Fuego,
Central America *could* be seen as the neck, the connector,
upon which hands *could* close,
cut by one slash, say, the Canal.

They would have to be big hands, hands used to
grabbing and clutching, well-exercised
and capable of crushing, holding on
past natural resistance.

Much damage occurs, there is a moment
when something in the eyes dull, but to this moment
there has been not a single case
of successful manual self-strangulation.

There is always a moment, and we must anticipate this,
when the grip loosens.

Always, if we can wait so long.

Porque los héroes nunca dijeron que morían por la patria,
sino que murieron.

— "Las casas quedaron llenas de humo"
Leonel Rugama

Because heroes never say they will die for their country,
they just die.

— "The houses were left filled with smoke"
Leonel Rugama

1.

Presente!
We remember!

2.

Nora Astorga just died.
Cancer.
Type not specified in the news
here in North America.
Left New York in December,
dying, left the people, in Nicaragua
in February, dead.

3.

Nora of the impassioned speeches.
Nora the elegant.
Nora of two years
in the heart of the enemy
beast, suffering
articles about the length

of her skirts, or which analyzed
the crossing of her knees
in the United Nations sessions,
and articles, self-serving articles
praising the old-world courtesies
of aging assassin generals, delegates
whose sclerotic meat swelled
to peep at this exotic enemy flower,
this enemy of their very own
priapic hegemony.

4.

Compañera.
Example of your people.
Example of a world.
Here in Canada the papers obsessed
about your ancient encounter
with one assassin general
half a generation ago. As if in a life
there was only one thing,
and then no more. Period.

The questions must have driven you crazy, *cara.*
After a speech in which you provided devastating
proof of violations of internal and international laws
by this nation full of generals, the first questions:
Were you naked when they killed the general?
Were you in the bedroom?
Had there been previous penetration?

Did you laugh bitterly, remembering
the grainy photo of the tearful Virgin of Matagalpa
a fresh icon from the fridge
in the humid cathedral?

5.

The 8 a.m. mention of your death on CBC Radio Regina,
squeezed between items on free trade between the U.S. and
Canada and on the efforts of your sweating country to reduce
hyperinflation imposed by those among whom you spent the last
two years.
Attempts to deal with this abstract economic cancer
with which your body politic has been inoculated. Watching
the *cordoba* metastasize, one split to twenty, 20 to 20,000. The price
of a single aspirin growing too heavy to carry without help.

Economy as poison, as bad cell, as foreign invader.

6.

We never met. Someone told me once that that was your head
I saw across the airport lounge.

7.

I kick at the snow as I walk up a small hill here in Saskatchewan,
Canada, more or less a full astronomical unit from your tomb. The
sound of my feet in the powdery snow, I swear, is "nora, nora, nora."
I kick at the snow as I walk down the hill again, and it is *"presente,
presente, presente."* I swear this is true. Try and disprove it.

8.

Nicaragua, Nicaraguita, the most beautiful flower of desire
sung in memory by Godoy.

The same song, sweeter and slower, sung in memory by Billy Bragg.

The same song, whispered by me at the foot of the small hill.

This hill is your tomb, your monument as much as any other.

Nora Astorga, proudly one of many.

Eternally *presente*.

9.

Listen:

"*Las generaciones venideras*
de la Nicaragua libre y luminosa
van a recordarte eternamente."

Generations to come
in free, in shining Nicaragua
will always
remember you.

Softly

and more softly

love.

The Distance Between The Fifteenth Of January, 1970 And The Tenth Of May, 1975

okay, say the task is to compare and contrast:

Leonel met death as every hero dreams – against overwhelming odds, pinned down, cameras rolling, two comrades already fallen, no way out, and coining a slogan that would squeeze a reverential laugh and tear from thousands for decades.

Roque, on the other hand, fell in a way which could be the sickest of fever dreams for any man – from behind, by the hands of his fellow revolutionaries, betrayed, smeared with the shit of induced CIA rumours, his compatriot assassins bringing shame and ridicule and shame not just to their faction, but to the dream of which Roque was a part, a shudder of horror to *el pueblo*.

light to darkness, *que se rinde tu madre* eroding the dragon's castle, *Roque fue asesinado* causing the dragon to laugh, propelling burst after burst of metal laughter into the crowds.

did Roque think of the books he had published?
did Leonel regret the lack of even one slim volume?

there is no evidence Leonel ever set foot in an airplane, nor any record of just how many air miles Roque logged across Mexico, Europe, Havana, North VietNam.

there is only a slim possibility, as thin as the finest sliver of imagination, that Roque's last flight back to El Salvador indeed violated the airspace above Leonel's three-year-old Nicaraguan grave. It is stretching it to believe that Roque slept, and dreamed of a squat *indio* skull set in a tragic smile, then woke for the descent into San Salvador.

it is a slim possibility.

such a conjunction
of culture and state
Rigoberto saw:
six empty chambers –
year among others

McCarthy in decline
nuclear explosions
year 23 of one man's rule
year in which he died
year before 1957

to make of my nation something beautiful
and leaderless
however briefly
is worth whatever sacrifice

six empty chambers
an empty chair
a notebook half full of poems
half empty of poems

so simple
a poem to his mother
like so many others
explaining
three shots from a pistol
and how to be beaten to death
in front of the warm corpse
of the dictator

I never met Julio when he was in the country. He would come in and meet with Borge and others, and word would filter down to us that Cortazar had been here again.

We would smile and look at each other, just the news buoying us up.

I never really knew much about the rest of his life, where he lived or what he did, what else he supported, what he attacked, I mostly knew him as a supporter of *la causa*, and I read several of his books, which were brilliant according to many, and it is true I found them so.

One thing which I treasured above much else was a note in his handwriting thanking me for the sheaf of poems I had sent him, which he said he had read with a warm and loving appreciation.

I do not know if it is true that the bastards infected him with the disease. I do not know if he really did die of a strange disease which caused his body to convince itself to grow younger and younger until his seventy-year-old heart could not stand it.

I would often unfold the grimy piece of paper and read it by the light of a match or whatever I might be using at the time.

INVESTIGATIVE LOSS

how it was lost,
how it got taken away,
how it was absorbed.

how it disappeared in the night,
how it was erased from the tape, just
how the signal was scrambled,
how the image was lost,
how it faded away.

how it got carried off,
how it was arrested and jailed,
how it fell into a hole in the earth,
how it was here no more,
how it got hidden,
how it evaporated,
how it melted away.

how mine wasn't there,
how yours was misplaced,
how it slipped her mind,
how no one knows where it is,
how there is no map,
how no message was left,
how there is no address,
how there is no number,
how thin air swallowed it up,
how it might be among papers,
how it was just here one minute ago.

how it is covered up,
how someone might have taken it away,
how it came to be other than where it was.

How there is a sense of loss.

It is easier to die than to remember.
- Briggflatts
Basil Bunting

During the course of composition I undertake to play only audio
tapes made during my times in Nicaragua.
I paper the walls with photos taken in the countryside.
I read only books published in the region.
I reduce my diet to *moros y cristianos*, black beans and rice, enforce
occasional shortages.
I monkey with the hot water tank so it only produces sporadic luke-
warm flows at inconsistent pressure.
I turn the heat way up.
I burn small pieces of car tire and corn flour in heavy oil for the
smell.
I dig out the white cotton collarless shirts and a pair of battered
running shoes.
I sweat heavily, tearing the filters off my cigarettes, buy bad coffee,
adding too much sugar.

I refuse to talk to Jo-Anne in anything but Spanish or heavily-
accented, truncated English.
I sneak around the house in the dark and spraypaint cryptic slogans
on the walls.
I hunch over the shortwave, searching in matchlight for an elusive
signal.
I curse the static.
I curse the regime which has reduced me to this.
I curse the dark.
I curse the heat, and the humidity, and the lack.
I curse the acrid smell of rebellion, and the sharp reek of the neces-
sity of it.

I do not have long now.
I hear the helicopter, the truck brakes, the shouted orders,
the furtive footfalls below the windows, the crackle of the field
radio.

This is no longer a safe house.

A poem hammers heavily on the door.

My toes start first. The pain ravages up my legs, flickers up one, then the other, they wither and twitch. Only when I feel the fire singe – oh god – my balls do I realize that I am not a short, stocky, gregarious writer. I am a *cordoba*. What the hell is going on? Instead of waiting around until it is Saturday to hear Nick Fillmore tell me I don't get an interview because of my lack of French, I am writhing in some fiery agony that is still moving up my body, now parboiling the half-digested contents of my gut.

I am not alone. I find my eyes, which, squeezed shut as I hurt, can only swivel side by side in the face of Augusto Cesar Sandino in one-third profile. There are others. Many others – millions, maybe billions of others, some of whom I can see swivelling their eyes from side to side in the faces of Carlos Fonseca, General Zeledon, Ruben Dario and so many, so many Sandinos. There is so much smoke.

I am consumed. I become the ashy motes that rise past yet more millions of Sandinos, mixing with the motes of so many others. We rise in particulate agony, from some pit that smells of ancient fire, twisting past those of us yet to burn, passing their fixed stares that do not know, they do not know, they will, and swirling, we rise round figures in three dimensions, figures of a woman in Presidential sash, figures of men in U.S. military costumes, they loom round the pit and watch us burn.

There is applause, there are handshakes all around us as we continue to rise and dissipate into the heated air. That is an end to us. I swim through air currents, and an untellable time later, am inhaled by a man at a desk. He coughs sharply, and stops writing.

I have no idea what to say.

It's Like

It's like someone walked into the bathroom
and said no I don't want you to shit that way, I
don't like that song you're playing, I don't like that
tune and leans over puts greasy bad smell over your
shoulder against the wheel and says no you're doing it all
wrong, there's a right way and a wrong way and you're
wrong about the way to breathe in, you go like this, forming
a circle with his lips and breathing out, saying this is
when you're all alone in the blackness a voice cuts
across the fantasy about her you've built carefully for
not the story about the old lady,
that's not the point,
it's the little dog that shat in the way of the wheelchair, he says,
puts his hand over yours and says no, son, that's not it,
and you want him to fall down with a heart attack because
you built it all by yourself and when he sits in it, it
goes all lopsided and he stands up and someone else sits and
pulls the tie around your neck twice and you choke as his fat
fingers pull the same strand tight it's simple, just do this he
says to her it's time for dictation no sit in this chair
over here and you feel his eyes like lumpy binoculars up your
eyes start to flame as the man steps up and plucks the
ballot from your hand and puts a mark on it that invalidates
all you have ever tried to do.

A Small Lesson In Stellar Physics

I got up this morning, climbed the hill as the sun rose over it, stared into that perfect circle, and spoke out loud a foreign name which had never before been spoken in all of human history there, which might never be spoken again.

Leonel.

The sun is a centre
of a poem, perhaps
what we wrap poems round.

93 million miles away
my small capsule of sound
did not achieve escape velocity,
never passed Venus,
never touched the crest
of the largest stellar flare.

Leonel.

It dispersed
as wave-forms do
spreading out past
the missile base in Alaska
past the missile base
in imprisoned Chile
past nuclear subs of the Pacific
past nuclear subs of the Atlantic
which, indeed, cost a lot of money.

Here in this province
one word of a poem
with which to wrap that sun
impossibly

we shall not say
we will throw this missile
from the barricades
around our death

we just will,
won't we,
Leonel?

Tanks have surrounded the Parliament Buildings in Ottawa, the Prime Minister's residence is under siege by heavily-armed men in civilian clothes, Cardinal Carter has been shot in the face and the heart while delivering the Easter homily and is presumed dead, there are currently thirteen mayors being held hostage, the border community of Prescott has been attacked, oil storage tanks in Kingston have been blown up, three Oshawa union leaders have been found with signs of torture, there are several unidentified body parts in the local waste disposal site, the offices of the *Toronto Star* were firebombed again today for the third consecutive day, no one has seen the head of the CBC for weeks and speculation is rife, the group entered the town of Belleville from the north shortly before midnight and gathered together the women and children and men separately, shot randomly into the crowds and raped a number of women before performing atrocities upon their bodies, the military has ordered University of Toronto and York closed indefinitely with no explanation, the OPP travelled from Wawa to Moosonee rounding up young men and pressing them into service hunting down those who have fled, crops are burning near Chatham, sporadic small arms fire is heard as this is typed, it is a normal day, it is an election day, U.S. media reports that an overwhelming number of us have expressed our confidence in the system.

WON'T TALK TO YOU

Because it is too far
you notice a bad smell in the shower
the host tastes of oil
the beer is skunky
meat gone rancid in the freezer
boiling stomach after your meal
of tainted soup
birds peck at the window
pigeons don't walk away
you see two cops
staring at each other

Because it is too far
traditional leaders continue to govern
despite quiet rectal cancer

men are found living in communes
behind prison bars, having abandoned
proprietary rights to exclusionary concepts

there is change beyond the meniscus
of a sloppy horizon
phonebooths suddenly emanate evil calls
surveillance machines fail

Because it is so far
movies become banal in transit
magazines are bought up
by Alcan, Anaconda, United Brands

your mother defends her small pile
of nothing
your brother grows hair
to breed ticks for sale
to university laboratories

because death in Central America
can only be "death in Central America"
no one will talk to you at work
there are more and more people
unemployed in your dreams
wasting away at cerebellic corners
try and convince your cats
there is more to life
than food

♦

I carry this picture so I will never forget

KEEP LOOKING

across the map of Nicaragua
Leonel walking

and walking
he is not in any one place
because he has already passed through it

like a conundrum

hills, and the labour of breath
leading up to them

and the economic fact
of buying one
book

a map
is one of the most expensive
things to print
to develop

when heroes and martyrs
abound
there is yet another colour added
to any map

and the *trompe-l'oeil*
by which it is easy to miss
Leonel traversing
mere geography

one big
ex-*here*

not any one place
but the place
and time
echoed

a point

a crux

From the audiographic headquarters in Miami/wave after wave of sound investigators to the hot spots/under special dispensation to investigate the sounds made with the body in confinement/& subjected to stimulation of pain centres/not subject to consideration of subject continuity

rub skin patch raw with sandpaper or a belt sander/RECORD

drip sulphuric acid onto patch/RECORD

spread legs of defiant being to form right angle at 45 degrees to body axis/one straight row of men in fatigues, cocks out erect/RECORD at 30-second intervals/dual mike/one taped to throat with black half-inch electrical tape one at male subject head level intercut same mike lowered at 45-second intervals to pelvic region victim/close-up/first man through fifth man/ensure mike 2 at male head level to capture the gutturals at ejaculation/RECORD

having come the men kick it to death/RECORD

machine pistol semi-auto to child's head/mike out of line of fire taped to skin/RECORD/PLAYBACK 10% real-time speed

mike to skin of subject denied food sixth week/RECORD

implant mike in family unit body cavity/beat body with blunt object/variant speed/RECORD

break bones in series/RECORD

slit throat/RECORD

PLAYBACK IN SLEEP

rough mix
PLAYBACK from satellite broadcast system
PLAYBACK alpha rhythm sync

loop it

REAL TIME

Why Me

there are so many
others

take them
if it does not matter
if it is all the same

take them

no

take me

THE CORPSE

I stood and watched one more word crawl out of his mouth, and I had to turn away. The head rested in a vast puddle of words, the smell was beyond belief, and the body still heaved and twisted with the words struggling to escape. By the time I turned to look again, the corpse was smothered in them, small colonies moving off in tiny bursts of sound.

TAPE SEGMENT

collected noise
breath burst over
inset mike

thunder
over cannonfire

they burn tires
to attract attention
used to be for meetings
still is

loud breath bangs
across years
speaks of smell
of burning tires

so acrid
so attractive

CIA INFLUX

when manipulation is a virtue
when Detroit automobiles are trademark of deathsquads
when pictures are altered
when the record is twisted
when the phonecall is never made
when the lifeforce is diminished
when there is a decision you are not allowed to make
when everything you say can and will be used against you
when you have seen the 50th murder on television, the 5000th, the
            six millionth
when they are denied
when papers are signed but not admitted to and burned after signing
when the patriot is burned after signing
when uniforms are in season
when dictators are forced to admit wrongdoing
when you know it is to cover up something immeasurably worse
when you know there are going to be another hundred headless
            bodies in the morning
when you know it will not be reported
when you know it cannot be stupidity and carelessness produces
            the bodycount, or the variances
when you know someone like you sat down and invented each torture
when you know there is not one atom cannot be made to disappear
when you know there is

no limit
no end
no taste
no higher power
no pity
no judgement
no discretion
no desire
no sense involved

what then
Mister Write-About-It?

Begin reciting the list of names, pacing round a simple wooden chair. At random, sit, tie one leg to the chair, then the other, then one arm, use other arm to pull canvas hood over head, use mouth to finish tying last arm, lean forward and with bound hand pull canvas hood tight. Continue reciting names through the hood. As the list goes on tip chair slowly backward using toes of bound feet, at your own name kick back to topple chair over backward. As chair lands, stop speaking.

Well Thank God That Is Done

I could be downstairs watching television, or making
my mind a blank until and if the postman delivers
the unemployment cheque in time for me to cash it
before or after a two o'clock appointment with
Jo-Anne's dentist for a cleaning and check-up
which is the only real event written in my
leather-covered daytimer datebook for today.

I could be drinking and thus oblivious to the
subtle irreversible changes in my liver as it
accumulates fat to scar and die.

I could be eating chocolate ice cream obsessively
and thinking about exercise on a regular basis.

I even could be ploughing through a well-used Spanish
English dictionary in a quest for a reason to go to
Nicaragua again, to drink (see above) and pass out
and be stripped and beaten in the pathetic excuse
for an alley two *cuadras* north of and around the
corner from where the dog pissed against the tree
because I supported in some manner unclear to me
the Sandinista Front for National Liberation to
which Rugama delivered the favour of his life
within vomiting distance from where I had hours
before seen colourful murals being erased by civil
servants of the new U.S. government

bringing remnants of a loyal army to tears.

OR FORGET IT

Once you have read this,
forget it.
It goes on and on about
forgotten fates of
forgotten writers in
forgotten countries, victims of
forgotten crimes, in a
forgotten region, during a
forgotten decade, once trendy for
forgotten reasons.

It was long ago
and far away
and besides
it is now said that then
we thought way beyond our means
and now the bill
has come due, for
someone's children,
somewhere, we've got to
tighten our thinking caps,
think only what we can afford to,
cut back wherever possible,
reduce our expectations
of thought, take pride
in less.

Let's just forget it
all, okay,
and move on.

III.
LEONEL

PREFACE

All of Leonel's work has been translated, and is in print today. All 60 pages of it. Fifteen poems and one polemic. One book. First published eight years after his death. If he had lived, he'd be a year older than me.

The following single poem from *The Earth is a Satellite of the Moon* is presented as a memorial. Its 90 lines encompass 500 years of history.

THE BOOK OF THE HISTORY OF CHE

Leonel Rugama (1949 – 1970)   *translation by Jim Smith*

The book of the history of CHE
child of Augusto
child of Lautaro
> *Inche Lautaro*
> *apubim ta pu huican*
> (I am Lautaro who fought the Spaniards)
husband of Guaconda
brother to Caupolica (archer of the sky)
and of Colocolo
begat Oropello;
Oropello begat Lecolon
and his brothers;
Lecolon begat Cayeguano;
Cayeguano begat Talco;
Talco begat Rengo;
Rengo begat Tupac-Amaru;
Tupac-Amaru begat Tupac-Yupanqui;
Tupac-Yupanqui begat Tucapel;
Tucapel begat Urraca of Panama;
Urraca begat Diriangen of Nicaragua
who committed suicide
in the foothills of the Casitas volcano
rather than be captured;
Diriangen begat Adiact
who was hanged
from a tamarind branch in Subtiava
here died the last indian chief
and the foreigners came to see this great thing.
Adiact begat Xochitl Acatl (flower of the cane)
Xochitl Acatl begat Guegue Miquistl (Old Dog)
Guegue Miquistl begat Lempira;
Lempira begat Tecun-Uman
Tecun-Uman begat Moctezuma Iluicamina;
Moctezuma Iluicamina begat Moctezuma Zocoyotizin;

Moctezuma Zocoyotizin begat Cuauhtemoc;
Cuauhtemoc begat Cuauhtemotizin
who was hanged by Cortez' men
and who said
> *Thus have I known*
> *how to value*
> *your false promises*
> *oh Malinche (Cortez)!*
> *I knew from the moment*
> *I did not die*
> *by my own hand*
> *when you entered my city*
> *of Tenochtitlan*
> *that this destiny was reserved for me.*

Cuauhtemotizin begat Quaupopoca;
Quaupopoca begat Tlacopan;
Tlacopan begat Huascar;
Huascar begat Geronimo;
Geronimo begat Gray Feather;
Gray Feather begat Crazy Horse;
Crazy Horse begat Sitting Bull;
Sitting Bull begat Bolivar;
Bolivar begat Sucre;
Sucre begat Jose de San Martin;
Jose de San Martin begat Jose Dolores Estrada;
Jose Dolores Estrada begat Jose Marti;
Jose Marti begat Joaquin Murrieta;
Joaquin Murrieta begat Javier Mina;
Javier Mina begat Emiliano Zapata;
Emiliano Zapata begat Pancho Villa;
Pancho Villa begat Guerrero;
Guerrero begat Ortiz;
Ortiz begat Sandino;
Augusto Cesar Sandino
brother of Juan Gregorio Colindres

and of Miguel Angel Ortez
and of Juan Umanzor

and of Francisco Estrada
and of Socrates Sandino
and of Ramon Raudales
and of Rufus Marin
and when he spoke he said:
our cause shall triumph
because it is a just cause
because it is the cause of love
and other times would say:
I would much prefer to die
with the few who accompany me
because it is preferable
for us to die as rebels
than to live as slaves.
Sandino begat Bayo
husband of Adelita
father of the CHE
whose name was Ernesto.

1968/1969

IV.
ROQUE

THE FOOTBALL WAR
PREFACE

Virtually unknown in North America, El Salvador's Roque Dalton is revered in Latin America for his poetry, his popular histories, and his revolutionary zeal. His murder in May, 1975, by a fanatic faction of his own party accomplished what two previous death sentences by the Salvadoran regime could not.

The short, brutal outbreak of war between his country and its neighbour, Honduras, in the summer of 1969, has been consigned to the dustbin of regional history. Portrayed as an unfortunate consequence of the stereotypically-excessive Latin temperament, the "football war" was ostensibly a result of a sports rivalry which got out of hand following playoffs for the World Football Championship of 1970. Regrettable, embarrassing, an aberration best forgotten.

In the years since I first read a mention of the incident, I have been inclined to shake my head ruefully, mutter about the silliness of sports fans in general, and pass on to the more relevant issues of the region.

Dalton's cross-examination of history, excerpts from which are here translated as "The Football War," is unclassifiable – serial poem via media analysis, polemic screed via documentary. It is a unique example of what Ed Sanders terms "investigative poetry."

It is unlikely that Roque Dalton at the time of his death on May 10, 1975, had ever heard of Noam Chomsky. However, had Chomsky been a poet, he might have produced a document like "War is the continuation of politics by other means, and politics is merely quintessential economics," the original Spanish title.

WAR IS THE CONTINUATION OF POLITICS BY OTHER MEANS AND
POLITICS IS MERELY QUINTESSENTIAL ECONOMICS
Roque Dalton (1935 – 1975)   *translation by Jim Smith*

1. Tegucigalpa, Honduras 25 May 1969 (AP) – The Honduran
Foreign Affairs Minister, speaking about the effects of Central
American economic integration on his country, pointed out that
Salvadoran-produced Colgate toothpaste is a major factor in the
increase of cavities among Honduran children.

2. San Salvador, El Salvador 26 May 1969 (UPI) – El Salvador's
Sub-Secretary of Economic Integration responded angrily to
Honduran accusations about the alleged poor quality of some
Salvadoran products imported by Honduras by pointing out that
Glostara hair cream, made in Honduras, produces dandruff.

3. Managua, Nicaragua 27 May 1969 (AFP) – Honduran and
Salvadoran ambassadors here each accused the other of serving a
"dictatorship" and of being agents of the economic aggression per-
petrated by each country on the other. Honduras accuses El
Salvador of shipping huge quantities of contraband fake whiskey to
Honduras. El Salvador accuses Honduras of introducing into the
Central American Common Market Belgian-made shirts with
Honduran labels, in order to destabilize the Salvadoran clothing
industry.

4. Mexico 27 May 1969 (AP) – Ex-President of Honduras, Dr.
Ramon Villeda Morales, declared to Associated Press that
Salvadoran industry, backed by powerful foreign monopolies, was
attempting to destroy the nascent Honduran industrial base in
order to supplant it in the Central American Common Market.
Alluding to Honduras' traditional role of food and agricultural sup-
plier, the Ex-President (commonly known as "Little Parrot"
throughout Central America) advised Salvadorans "Do not bite
the hand that feeds you."

5. Guatemala City, Guatemala 28 May 1969 (AFP) –U.S. ambassadors and their military attachés in Guatemala, El Salvador, Honduras, Nicaragua and Costa Rica met for three days in Guatemala in order to consult with high-level State Department and Pentagon authorities about the Central American situation. They refused to divulge the substance of their meetings, which they termed "routine."

6. Havana, Cuba 30 May 1969 (PL) – Cuba's official paper *Granma* points out the unnatural aspect of Central American economic integration – all five national economies of the region are competitive, not complementary. Each one competes in the world market with their coffee, bananas or sugar; this competition is made worse by their attempts to dominate the Common Market with their industrial production. Central American integration – according to *Granma* - can only benefit imperialism.

7. San Salvador 30 May 1969 (*La Prensa Grafica*) – The Central American and Caribbean Football Confederation (CONCACAF) assigned dates for the playoffs between the national teams of Honduras and El Salvador to determine which of the two countries would take part in the final elimination round of the World Football League championship, to take place in Mexico in 1970.

8. "Central America's Social Problems" (Editorial in *Student Opinion*, San Salvador) – For a number of reasons (the 1932 massacre, land evictions, chronic unemployment, hunger) a huge stream of refugees flows outward from El Salvador. More than 35 thousand live in San Francisco; in Mexico, over 60 thousand, most illegally; in Guatemala, some 75 thousand. In Honduras the Salvadoran population has grown to more than 350 thousand, mostly poor *campesinos*, nervously occupying unworked land in underpopulated Honduras.

9. A Love Poem

Those who dug out the Panama Canal
those who washed up from the Pacific fleet
on California shores
those putrefying in the jails of Guatemala,
Mexico, Honduras, Nicaragua
as thieves, smugglers, crooks,
as greedy,
those always suspected of everything
("allow me to bring forth the accused,
found on a suspicious corner,
Salvadoran to boot")
those who fill the taverns and bordellos
of every port and capital in the zone
("The Blue Grotto," "Little Britches," "Happyland")
sowers of corn in every foreign field,
kings of debt,
those who don't know anyone else wherever they are,
best craftsmen in the world,
those who were stitched with bullets on crossing the frontier,
those who died of malaria,
or of the scorpion sting or yellow spider bite
in the hell of the banana plantation,
those who cried drunkenly at the national anthem
under the Pacific cyclone or the snows of the north,
the strikers, the beggars, marijuanistas,
worm children of the big whore,
those who almost came home,
those who had a little more luck,
the eternally documentless,
the do-it-alls, the sell-it-alls, the eat-it-alls,
the ones on the tip of the knife,
the saddest of the sad of the world,
my compatriots,
my brothers.

10. *Tricontinental Review*, 1969 – "According to General Westmoreland, top U.S. theorist in special warfare, speaking at a conference of the highest military chiefs of Latin America recently held in Rio de Janeiro: 'Heightening the prestige of the native Armed Forces is absolutely indispensable to the United States continental goal of anticommunist counter-insurgency.'"

11. *Information for the Tourist*: El Salvador has an area of 21,292 square kilometres and a population of 3 million, 750 thousand persons. Honduras covers 141,521 square kilometres with a population of 2 million, 250 thousand persons. Thus Honduras has a population density of 15 people per square kilometre to El Salvador's 178. President of Honduras is General Oswaldo Lopez Arellano, who received his education in North American military academies. President of El Salvador is General Fidel Sanchez Hernandez, who received his education in North American military academies, and who served as a United Nations North American observer in the Korean conflict and is Ex-President of the Inter-American Defence Council.

12. Guatemala, 31 May 1969 (dispatch by the visiting correspondent of London's *The Economist*) – International commentators see signs of optimism for the Central American region; El Salvador's Sanchez government has overcome, using only limited violence, nearly two years of strikes unparalleled on a national scale in nearly forty years; and since then the Guatemalan military government has provided assurances of having liquidated the revolutionary movement which has disquieted this land of eternal spring. In Honduras, the Arellano government terminated definitively and with force an agrarian peasant movement that could have tended toward violent forms of struggle, inflaming liberal opposition to the more rightist sector of the Armed Forces and increasing discontent among students and teachers, which might have been translated into strikes and disturbances.

13. Official announcement by the President of Honduras – The Honduran government, in accordance with the spirit of the times and with attention to the size of the country, but without any alteration to our constitutionally democratic regime and with care to preserve the rights to private property and free enterprise, have decreed and ordered the implementation of Agrarian Reform in all national territory.

14. Monologue by a Honduran planner simultaneously progressive and adroit – "In order to bring to fruition the Agrarian Reform which the U.S. Alliance for Progress demands, we have to give up certain land. The *problem* is which lands to give up, specifically. To intrude on the properties of the North American United Fruit Company is taboo. If we touch the property of the Honduran upper class landholders we would be communist. To put a hand on the national forests would be too expensive. We are left, then, with the lands exploited by Salvadoran immigrants, about 370 thousand hectares. If we expropriate the worms, we will appear patriotic, grabbing back land for Hondurans out of foreign hands. That the United Fruit Company is also foreign, because they are Yankees? It won't come up. It's a simple arithmetic problem – the number of Salvadorans on our sovereign territory is about 300 thousand, while Yankee residents here are less than 3 thousand, and are helping us civilize ourselves. And also, it demonstrates our practical spirit: we will resemble the Yankee agrarian reformists by giving back land snatched from the Indians. And, finally, to demonstrate that we are radical, we will order the expropriation of the Salvadorans without any form of compensation."

15. Brilliant idea of a Honduran jurist – "In order to avoid giving land to Salvadorans resident in Honduras, it will suffice to apply article 68 of the Agrarian Reform law, establishing that only Hondurans by birth can be beneficiaries of the Reform. And, in order to get rid of the Salvadorans it will suffice to apply the Immigration Laws widely."

16. Poem

Laws are for the obedience
of the poor.
Laws are made by the rich
in order to instill a little order to exploitation.
The poor are the only obeyers of laws
of history.
When the poor shall make the laws
then, then there will be no rich.

17. Tegucigalpa, Honduras June 1969 – Honduras beat El Salvador two goals to one in the first match of the series which decides who participates in the world tournament. Honduran military and hundreds of car owners were situated the entire previous night out front of the hotel of the Salvadoran players, exploding skyrockets and blowing their horns so the team could not sleep and started play exhausted.

18. San Salvador, first week of June 1969 (editorial, *La Prensa Grafica*) – Well-known landholder and Salvadoran man of business, Don Atanasio Guirola Alvarez has made important declarations to our paper regarding the situation in Honduras. "Whatever the case in another country," – said Mr. Guirola – "for us, we are indifferent to agrarian reform. But I do not see why we should pay for the broken vessel of Honduran agrarian reform. If General Lopez Arellano wants to foment communistoid demagoguery, let him do it without burning his neighbours. If the 350 thousand Salvadorans who live productively in Honduras return to our country, unemployment will be multiplied by 350 thousand, and the national situation will be pushed to the edge of revolution. And this is what we must avoid. What will be will be." (This editorial was finally not published as the director of *La Prensa Grafica* considered it "inconvenient.")

19. Tegucigalpa, Honduras, first week of June (*El Dia*, early edition) – The Honduran Minister of Finance declares: "The illegal Salvadorans must depart from Honduras. El Salvador has to carry the weight of its own demographics."

20. San Salvador, first week of June, 1969 (*El Mundo*) – The President of the Institute for Industrial Development, engineer Gabriel Pons, states that the gravest problem suffered by El Salvador is that of unemployment, since of every three persons, two are without work.

21. Washington, 8 June 1969 (AP) – "From the military point of view," – stated before a congressional committee by General Theodore C. Handkerchief, Pentagon Special Operations Attaché – "the key link of our Central American security apparatus is the Honduran army. The Honduran military," – he added – "does not understand that we are living in the second half of the twentieth century."

22. San Salvador, 15 June 1969 (AFP) – News arriving from Honduras indicates that Honduran paramilitary forces, among them an ultra-rightist band known as "The Wild Bunch," is evicting by force from their small parcels of land hundreds of Salvadoran *campesinos* who had settled years ago in that country. There are numerous atrocities. Hundreds of Salvadoran families have begun to return to this country by way of the frontier, in what appears to be the beginning of a massive exodus which could, in the end, include the totality of the Salvadoran population residing in Honduras.

23. San Salvador, 16 June 1969 (PL) – The Salvadoran press has begun an intense campaign against the atrocities suffered in Honduras by Salvadoran residents who are being thrown off their land. *El Mundo* reports hundreds of Salvadorans assassinated, women raped by Honduran mobs and farmhouses burned down with the inhabitants trapped inside. *El Mundo* included an inter-view with a Salvadoran woman who arrived on foot from Honduras, crossing forests and rivers, and whose both breasts were cut off by elements of the "The Wild Bunch." *El Mundo* is a semi-official paper of an anonymous society to which belong many important figures in the Sanchez government.

24. San Salvador, 17 June 1969 (AFP) – The national press is unanimous in its demand of the Sanchez government: "You must take drastic measures against Honduras."

25. Washington, 20 June 1969 – El Salvador accuses Honduras of "genocide by expulsion." Honduras denies the charges and accuses El Salvador of preparing for an aggressive act of its own. Costa Rica, Guatemala and Nicaragua have offered their good offices to help solve the conflict. There are reports of sporadic clashes between Salvadoran and Honduran border patrols. There are rumours among generally well informed circles that a breakdown of diplomatic relations between the two countries is imminent.

26. San Salvador 23 June 1969 (UPI) – In San Salvador's National Stadium, the Salvadoran team defeated the Honduran team two goals to one, tying the series which will determine participation in the World Finals. The Honduran players arrived at the Stadium in individual Volkswagens, each guarded by soldiers armed with machine guns, and were conducted in this way to the very edge of the playing field. The night before, groups of Salvadorans, headed by the Director of both Intelligence Services and the Salvadoran National Guard, General Jose Alberto Medrano (whom opponents of the regime accuse of being the top CIA man in the country),

attempted to create disturbances in front of the hotel where the Honduran players were staying in order to prevent them from sleeping. These disturbances widened, and finally the police shot at the curious onlookers. The final result was two unidentified citizens dead, and seven university students detained. A Molotov cocktail burned down a door of the Central Post Office, near the site of the disturbances. In the National Stadium several Hondurans who had come to cheer their team on were insulted and badly handled by groups of Salvadoran fans. When the orchestra played the Honduran national anthem, many Salvadoran fans hissed, booed and greeted the music with obscene hand gestures. The tie-breaking game will take place in a neutral location, presumably in Guatemala or in Mexico.

27. Decals for car windshields which were on sale in Tegucigalpa, Honduras at some commercial enterprises, including the North American business which manufactures and distributes Glostara hair cream: "Hondurans! Grab a stick, kill a Salvadoran!"

28. San Salvador, 25 June 1969 (AP) – El Salvador decides to break off diplomatic relations with Honduras. *El Mundo*, in an editorial, says that El Salvador must undertake the mission of civilizing Honduras by means of force. "Perhaps this is the destiny which Providence has endowed to El Salvador in Central America," – said the editorial written for the paper by its Director, lawyer, diplomat, poet and chronicler Waldo Chavez Velazco – "like that given to Israel amidst the fearsome Arab world."

29. Reflection of an old Salvadoran writer, a liberal-democratic opposition member, famous locally for his sarcasm: "So now it has to be that El Salvador is the people picked by God to force Central America to progress by balls or by fire. And it is said that we are the Israelites of the isthmus and the Hondurans are the Arabs. And that our Moshe Dayan is the General Fidel Sanchez. It isn't dead, but its dwarfish. Something is something, all right."

30. San Salvador, 30 June 1969 (AFP) – The exodus of Salvadorans from Honduras has intensified noticeably. Information from official sources indicates that more than 75 thousand of the Salvadorans have already returned to our national territory and that the rhythm of the exodus has been increasing hourly. The well-known landholder and industrialist, Don Emeterio Regalado Borghi, in statements that were not published by the local press, declares: "The hour of the rifle has come. We either fire them against the government of Honduras or we will very soon have to fire them at the Salvadorans who overflow in this country."

31. San Salvador, 1 July 1969 (*Student Opinion*) – Señora Carmen de Lopez testified before the Supreme Court that her husband, the well-known union leader Alberto Lopez, was snatched and held prisoner by a group of men armed with machine-guns in a car without plates, who then denounced him in loud voices as being a Honduran spy. Lopez was wounded by a bullet while trying to escape, and his wife fears for her life.

32. San Salvador, 5 July 1969 (*Student Opinion*) – Deputy to the Legislative Assembly of the National Reconciliation Party, Dr. Juan Dono Altamirano, accompanied by a group of armed men, spread terror in the Barrio Panamericana, grabbing a number of secondary school and university students and attempting to shoot them in a nearby ravine, due to the accusation that they were Hondurans who were dedicated to giving poisoned caramels to Salvadoran children. Neighbours and fathers from nearby families prevented the shooting. Government Deputy Dono Altamirano did not exhibit signs of having ingested alcohol or heroic drugs.

33. San Salvador, 13 July 1969 (AP) – North Americans landed on the moon; because of this, the news of the conflict with Honduras was displaced from the front pages of the San Salvador newspapers. In an address to the nation, the Salvadoran President commented: "It is safer to walk on the moon than on the sidewalks of Honduras."

34. Honduras was invaded by Salvadoran troops on two fronts. San Salvador was blacked out in anticipation of an attack by Honduran warplanes.
Bloody combat was reported in the frontier zones.
The Salvadoran Army advanced rapidly.
Air combat unseen since the days of WW2.
The Salvadoran strategy – occupy territory in order to force negotiations.
Paradox of war – reports of more civilian deaths than military.
Washington states it will intervene in the Organization of American States to impose peace.
Marxist organizations in Honduras and El Salvador provide assistance "critically" to their respective governments and call for national unity against their respective enemy.
The Salvadoran Army occupies extensive territory in Honduras.
Headline in a Salvadoran daily – "We have to push through to the Atlantic!"
Small article in a Salvadoran daily – "We haven't been stopped? Something is rotten in the state of Denmark!"
Salvadoran university students are called up to defend their homeland.
Honduran university students as well.
A tiny group of med students and a doctor, ex-rector of the university: the only persons who maintain in El Salvador that the war is a ploy of the dominant classes and of U. S. imperialism. The Salvadoran Army within 75 kilometres of Tegucigalpa, Honduras.
The Organization of American States calls for a ceasefire.
Salvadoran troops will only retire under the assurance that the

350 thousand Salvadorans would be allowed to stay (or return, in some cases) in Honduras permanently.

"But this has to happen quickly," – insists the well-known Salvadoran landholder Don Mario Duenas Meza – "because those expelled have become mountains. They must be stopped immediately as well. If the war enters a period of negotiations and this prolongs it, we will have to stop with bullets these ungrateful Salvadorans who until now knew where they belonged and who now want to come back here to snatch food out of our children's mouths."

A delegation from the Organization of American States arrives in El Salvador and Honduras.

The Salvadoran government initiates a huge public fundraising campaign in order to purchase new weapons outside the country: they sell a bond issue called "Bonds of National Dignity."

The average Honduran infantry soldier utilizes a bolt-action Springfield rifle, like that used in the First World War. The Salvadoran soldier uses the G-3 automatic rifle of recent West German manufacture, with clips of 20 or 30 bullets.

The first Salvadoran soldiers to return home to the capital from the battlefield, rejoicing, are received as heroes.

The Organization of American States proposes a negotiated solution.

The Salvadoran government accuses the Honduran government of being communist and of receiving aid from Fidel Castro and Guatemalan guerrillas.

The Honduran government accuses the Salvadoran government of being communist and of receiving aid from the Guatemalan guerrillas and from the Nicaraguan guerrillas.

The way in which soldiers have returned from the field of battle to the Salvadoran capital has given rise to rumours among the population of the cowardice of officers in combat and of atrocities committed against the civilian population of Honduras. Thus all leaves have been cancelled, and all diversions for troops will take place in the vicinity of the field of battle. With this in mind, the

Logistics Branch of the Salvadoran Army has commenced executing operation "Moonlight," which features among other amusements and diversion, the dispatch of 850 Salvadoran prostitutes to the front.

Both armies accept a ceasefire. Negotiations are commencing for their withdrawal.

35. Some Questions

"El Salvador accuses the government of Lopez Arellano of genocide. The Salvadoran government, with the assistance of the Red Cross and with the effective support of the people, offers to these refugees immediate help: by giving them food and assistance for one or two days maximum, and then disperses them throughout the country, on the pretext of taking them to their places of origin...If the government has been incapable of solving the problems of the first 17 thousand persons who returned from Honduras, what solution can they offer after the return of one or two or three hundreds of thousands of Salvadorans?" Luis Fuentes Rivera, *The Honduras-El Salvador Conflict*, 1969.

"Why did the government of El Salvador decide to invade Honduras instead of waiting for the decision of the Human Rights Commission of the Organization of American States?" *op. cit.*

("...the position of the Organization of American States was not favourable to El Salvador, and they had no intention of declaring Honduras guilty of genocide, but would have taken some concrete measures to restrain the return of the Salvadorans; in effect, the decision given down by the Human Rights Commission was more critical of El Salvador than Honduras; it condemned the passivity of the governments to solve the problems arising from the football competition, and above all would have criticized the government of El Salvador, where these disturbances were much more serious, and also would have condemned the government of this country for not having taken efficient steps to make unnecessary the migration of Salvadorans to Honduras in the first place; that is to say, criticize the internal conditions of El Salvador which caused the migration...") *op. cit.*

"An important fact: during the week of war, Salvadoran radio (apart from transmitting some erroneous information about which cities were taken) was constantly calling for Salvadorans resident in Honduras to "fulfil their debt"; that is to say, to commit sabotage and to aid the Salvadoran troops; this included a station inside Honduras (supposedly managed by Salvadorans) which made such calls to action. A request of this sort, in a war situation, is nothing more or less than an invitation to Hondurans to double their persecution and revenge against the Salvadorans resident in Honduras; a call, in effect, for their eradication. If the war was made in order to defend the lives and property of the Salvadorans resident in Honduras, how can one understand this appeal for self-destruction? How would this unarmed civilian population be able to fight against the Honduran army? The only true objective was to impede these Salvadorans from ever returning to their country – they could stay there or they could die, but never return?" *op. cit.*

As conditions for the withdrawal of troops from Honduran territory, El Salvador insisted that the government of Honduras must: a) guarantee the lives, property and right to remain of all Salvadorans in Honduras, b) punish those responsible for the outrages. It ended that the Salvadoran troops retired without these conditions being fulfilled. If El Salvador dominated the situation from the military point of view, and had publicly repudiated the position of the Organization of American States, what power caused the withdrawal of their troops?

Who, what power stood to make concrete gains as a result of the Honduran-Salvadoran conflict?

36. Reflection

There are no "mysteries of History."
There are only the falsifications of history
the lies of those who write History.
The History poorly named the "football war"
which had been written by the CIA and Pentagon
and the intelligence services of the governments
of El Salvador and Honduras
and the journalistic hacks of the oligarchies of both countries,
the publicity flacks of the industries of economic integration,
the public relations experts and the marketplace gods of the
      Central American suburb,
the prudent and totally anonymous editorialists
the chroniclers and the reporters
of the Established Press of the isthmus (including Radio and TV)
the Information Ministries and the Psychological Warfare Sections
of the Major States unified in the Central American Defence
      Agreement, etc., etc.,
the forgery of the history of this war
is merely the continuation by other means,
the continuation of the real war which continues
under the facade of a war between El Salvador and Honduras:
the imperialist-oligarchic-bourgeois-governmental war
against the peoples of Honduras and El Salvador.

37. Some Results of the Conflict (To Date)

Between 250-300 dead and a thousand wounded for each army. More than 5 thousand dead from the civilian population (the majority Honduran).

Various Honduran villages erased from the map by artillery and bazooka fire.

Hatred between two peoples traditionally fraternal.

Concentration camps for Salvadorans in Honduras.

Tens of thousands of Salvadorans harassed and expelled from their land.

The pillaging of Honduran villages captured by the Salvadoran Army.

Honduran citizens assassinated in El Salvador merely because of their citizenship.

Honduran and Salvadoran revolutionaries and opposition figures assassinated in each of the two countries on the accusation of being friendly to the "enemy."

20 million dollars admitted as the cost of military mobilization in each country (supplies, destroyed equipment, etc.).

Prolonged consolidation of both military dictatorships on the foundation of the call for national unity against the enemy of the homeland.

Reduction in the effectiveness of leftist organizations in both countries in the face of jingoist frenzy.

Internal divisions within leftist organizations of both countries concerning whether or not to offer assistance to their respective "national" governments.

Monopolistic concentration in numerous sectors of the industrial economy of El Salvador and Honduras after the collapse of any number of small enterprises unable to withstand the market uncertainty for their products during the rupture of Salvadoran-Honduran commercial relations.

The theft of the major part of the money obtained from the public appeal to fund the buying of arms (by means of the public issue of

"Bonds of National Dignity"), committed by the highest functionaries of the Sanchez Hernandez regime in El Salvador. The fraction of the money raised actually spent on arms went to buy helicopters and old weapons, mothballed as unserviceable from overflowing U.S. stockpiles.

The rearmament and modernization of the Salvadoran Army under U.S. supervision.

The modernization and rearmament of the Honduran Army under U.S. supervision.

Reinforcement of the U.S. military presence and U.S. security and intelligence services throughout Central America.

Major penetration of U.S. agencies in the state apparatus of both countries, by way of plans to assess emergency preparedness and to improve the level of technical instruction, etc.

Tremendous inflation of the prices of consumer items in both countries.

Militarization of the state and laws of Honduras and El Salvador: the Army converted to the instrument of fundamental repression and state planning, the source of the countries' international and national policy, the only source of power in the heart of the state, the power which specifies and sets the limits on individual and social rights.

Increased growth in unemployment in both countries and the decrease in both real salaries and their purchasing power.

Tens of thousands of Salvadorans wandering hungry from the mountains of Honduras to El Salvador, and from the mountains of El Salvador to Honduras.

In Honduras they have no land.

In El Salvador they have no land and no work.

They are neither Salvadorans nor Hondurans:

they are the poor.

barrio – *district*

bolsa – *bag, shopping bag*

calle – *street*

campesinos – *country people*

cerveza – *beer*

cese la represíon – *Stop the repression (fr. Salvadoran Archbishop Romero's letter to U.S. President Jimmy Carter shortly before Romero's assasination on orders of later U.S.-sponsored Arena Party presidential candidate Roberto D'Aubisson in 1980)*

comandantes – *a high rank in the revolutionary army*

compañeros – *companion, mate, close and trusted friends*

con un abrazo fuerte – *with a big hug*

cordoba – *basic unit of Nicaraguan currency (paper)*

cuadras – *blocks (along a street)*

dolor – *pain*

el muerto – *death*

el pueblo – *the people (collective)*

encuentro – *meeting*

finca – *ranch, farm*

fisicamente – *physically*

guardia – *the Guard (ie, National Guard-Somoza's army/police)*

hijo de puta – *son of a whore, son of a bitch*

indio – *indian, indian-like*

la causa – *"the cause", the revolution*

maiz – *corn*

masa – *dough*

matanza – *(the) killing (refers to the 1932 massacre in El Salvador of 30-50,000)*

mezcla – *mixture, jumble*

patron – *landlord, boss*

poemas – *poems*

presente! – *present (as in a roll-call response), always emphatic*

puta – *whore*

que se rinde tu madre – *literally, "surrender your own mother"; the regionally-famous epithet Leonel Rugama threw back in response to a request to give himself up shortly before his death*

quintal – *local unit of measure, roughly equivalent to a bushel*

ron – *rum*

Roque fue asesinado – *Roque has been assassinated*

15th January 1970 – date of Leonel Rugama's death

10th May 1975 – date of Roque Dalton's death

Augusto Cesar Sandino – took to the hills in Nicaragua with a small band of followers in 1933; fought the U.S. Marines to frustration; assassinated by Somoza the Elder, having been tricked to come down from the hills to discuss peace; the S in FSLN

Bank of America building – sole highrise to survive the 1972 earthquake in Managua; dominates the landscape to date

Bartolomeo de las Casas – priest who chronicled the Spanish conquest of Central America and killing of millions

Billy Bragg – contemporary British folk/protest musician

Calvario Market – a marketplace in San Salvador, capital of El Salvador

Carlos Fonseca – founder, with Tomas Borge, of the FSLN; killed by the National Guard 8 November 1976

Cayetano Carpio – "Marcial"; Salvadoran revolutionary leader of the FPL

Cementerio La Bermeja – a cemetery on the edge of San Salvador

Chalatenango – a province and a city in El Salvador

Cine Altamirana – a rundown cinema and concert venue in Managua

Comandante Ana Maria – murdered 2nd-in-command of FPL

Del Fuego – Tierra del Fuego, the southernmost point of Latin America

Farabundo Marti – leader of the 1932 uprising in El Salvador, murdered in the massacre which followed; the FM in FMLN

FMLN – The Farabundo Marti Front for National Liberation (El Salvador)

FSLN – the Sandinista National Liberation Front (Nicaragua)

General Zeledon – 1912 leader of rebellion against U.S. troops of occupation in Nicaragua; predecessor to Sandino

Godoy (and *the brothers* Godoy) – Luis Enrique and Carlos Mejia; FSLN militants, best-known and loved musicians in modern Nicaragua; core of Guitarra Armada

Granma – the boat which carried Fidel Castro and his men to Cuba in 1956; honored in the name of Cuba's daily paper

Guitarra Armada – primary guerrilla music group in Nicaragua during the revolution; songs and tapes clandestine but widespread and popular

Julio Cortazar – novelist

Managua – oft-earthquaked capital city of Nicaragua

Matagalpa – small, dusty agricultural city in the mountains in the north of Nicaragua; cattle and coffee region

Mercado Oriental – Eastern Market; one of Managua's largest outdoor/indoor markets

Monroe Doctrine – Longstanding U.S. assertion of its destined dominance over all of Latin America

Mothers of the Disappeared – groups of mothers of disappeared in various Latin countries who confront authorities about the fate of their children

Museum of the Revolution – a small building near the Mercado Oriental in Managua

Nora Astorga – Sandinista combatant, unprecedentedly rejected as Nicaragua's ambassador to the U.S., Nicaragua then appointed her the country's ambassador to the United Nations

Pipil – one of the lesser-known indigenous groups of the Central American region; eradicated by the Spanish

Popol Vuh – one of the holy books of the indigenous peoples of Central America

Quiche – one of the lesser-known indigenous peoples of the region; now mainly in the highlands of Guatemala

Rigoberto Lopez Perez – Nicaraguan poet who in 1956 assassinated the first Somoza, then was beaten to death by guards

Rosario Murillo – Nicaraguan poet, wife of FSLN President Daniel Ortega, former head of Sandinista Association of Cultural Workers

Ruben Dario – Nicaragua's most famous poet of the late 19th-early 20th century

Sandino – see *Augusto Cesar Sandino*, above

San Jose – capital city of Costa Rica; haven for many Nicaraguan revolutionaries prior to their victory in 1979

San Salvador – capital of El Salvador

Tegucigalpa – capital of Honduras

The Archbishop – El Salvador's Archbishop Oscar Romero, assassinated while celebrating mass in 1980

Those giants in Masaya – folk dance using giant double-life-size puppets, folk satire of U.S. domination

Tienda La Trinidad – a run-down corner store in San Salvador

Tomas Borge – only surviving founder of Nicaragua's FSLN; Minister of the Interior 1980-1990 in the Sandinista government

Victor Jara – revered Chilean folk singer, killed in the first days of the coup against Salvador Allende in 1973; his extraordinarily long fine-boned hands were first crushed then cut off prior to his death in the stadium in Santiago, Chile

Wiwili – small village in the north of Nicaragua; site of some of the most vicious contra attacks on Nicaragua 1981-1990

My life partner, Jo-Anne McNamara, who nourished these poems, as she did the writer.

My dear friends Mindy Camponeschi (the cover artist) and Eugenio Tellez, painters extraordinaire, who blazed the path that took me to Nicaragua so many years ago.

Friend and mentor Gary Geddes, travelling companion and Canada's finest living political poet.

My dearest mother, who worried while I was away, and who died before this book could explain what I brought back.

My old friend Judy Merril, who always challenged me to explain myself.

My friend Douglas Young, who took a break from landscape architecture to take the photo of me.

The Ontario Arts Council from time to time, for grants in aid.

The good people at Curbstone Press in Willimantic, Connecticut, who provided permission for my translations of Roque and Leonel. They have published the following books by Roque and Leonel. Please seek them out and read them:

The Earth is a Satellite of the Moon – Leonel Rugama (trs.Miles/Schaaf/Weisberg)

Poemas Clandestinos/Clandestine Poems – Roque Dalton (trs. Hirschman)

Small Hours of the Night: Selected Poems of Roque Dalton (ed. St. Martin; trs. Cohen/Graham/ Nelson/Pines/St. Martin/Unger)

Miguel Marmol – Roque Dalton (trs. Ross/Schaaf)

Finally, for Charles Smith, my nephew.

ABOUT THE AUTHOR

J im Smith is an accomplished Toronto poet, journalist and editor. He has more than six books to his name, including *The Schwartz-negger Poems, Convincing Americans, Crinoid Hill, Translating Sleep,* and *100 Most Frightening Things.* His work has appeared in a number of anthologies, and he has over 100 periodical publication credits. He has done extensive translating of works by Latin American writers.

Jim Smith was born in Niagara Falls and grew up in Kingston, Ontario. He has an MA in Creative Writing from Concordia University in Montreal, and a law degree from Osgoode Hall. He currently lives in Toronto, and will be called to The Ontario bar in February, 1999.